Women

Win the

Vote

DATES WITH HISTORY

6 February 1918

Women
Win the
Vote

Brian Williams

CHERRYTREE
BOOKS

A Cherrytree Book

First published 2005
by Cherrytree Books, part of
Evans Brothers Limited
2a Portman Mansions
Chiltern Street
London W1U 6NR

VISIT OUR WEBSITE
Evans
www.evansbooks.co.uk

British Library Cataloguing in Publication Data

Williams, Brian
Women win the vote - (Dates with History)
1. Women - Suffrage - History - 20th Century - Juvenile
literature
1. Title
324. 6'23

ISBN 1842342576

Editor: Julia Bird
Designer: Mark Holt

Picture credits:

Corbis: Front cover, 7, 9, 11, 13, 17, 18
Mary Evans Picture Library: 6, 8, 10, 12, 22, 23, 25, 26, 27
Topham Picturepoint: 14, 15, 16, 19, 20, 21, 24

Contents

Women cast their votes

Today in Britain, all men and women over the age of 18 have the right to vote in elections to the British Parliament, the European Parliament and local councils. They have not always enjoyed this right. As recently as the 19th century, no women and only men with money or property could vote. 'Universal suffrage', or votes for all, was still a long way off.

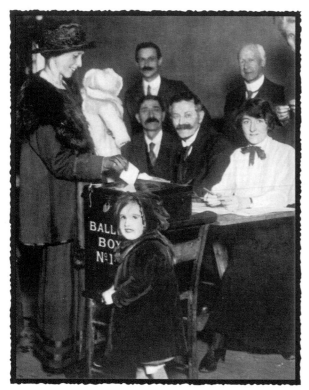

Women in Britain cast their first votes in the historic general election of 1918.

Change eventually came in 1918, when on 6 February a new law gave the vote to all men and to women over the age of 30. On 28 December 1918 women in Britain voted in a **general election** for the first time. So ended a long campaign by women from many different social backgrounds. The most active campaigners, known as suffragettes, had defied ridicule and public condemnation. Hundreds had gone to prison for their beliefs.

In the 1918 general election, there were only 17 women out of 1600 **candidates** to become Members of Parliament (MPs). But in 1919, Nancy Astor triumphantly entered the House of Commons as Britain's first woman MP, and in 1924 Margaret Bondfield became the first woman government minister. In 1979 Britain elected its first female prime minister, Margaret Thatcher. Today, there are more women in Parliament (119 out of a total of 659 MPs in 2004) than ever before.

Winning the vote in 1918 was a huge victory for women's rights after a long struggle. In 1928 the law was revised to give all women over 21 the vote. The voting age for both men and women was lowered to 18 in 1969.

Margaret Thatcher waves from number 10 Downing Street with her husband Denis, after victory in the 1979 general election makes her Britain's first female prime minister.

Peace after war

Women in Britain had always worked on farms and at home, but the **Industrial Revolution** of the 18th and 19th centuries changed the nature of the work they did. Many women took jobs in the new factories and textile mills, despite being paid less than male workers. Later on, women found jobs in the expanding business world, working in telephone exchanges and as clerks and typists. The largest group of women workers were **domestic servants** – there were two

Millions of men enlisted in the armed forces to fight in World War I. Women took over many men's jobs on the 'home front'.

million of them by 1911. Working allowed women more independence, but they had little or no say in running the country.

The lives of many women in Britain were irreversibly changed by the First World War, which broke out on 4 August 1914 and lasted for four years. Millions of men joined the army and hundreds of thousands of them were killed in battle. With so many men away fighting, women were forced to do men's work. By 1918, more than four million women were at work in factories, on farms and in hospitals.

This government poster urged women to do war work making munitions (weapons). In return, women expected fair treatment.

The 1914-18 war proved that women could do many jobs just as well as men. The post-war world was changing rapidly, with inventions such as the aeroplane, radio and cinema improving the quality of everyday life. Women wanted this change to extend to politics – they wanted to be allowed a say in their country's government.

The long struggle

In 19th-century Britain, most men and many women (including Queen Victoria, who reigned from 1837 to 1901) believed a woman's place was at home. They pointed to the history of great ancient civilisations. Women in ancient Greece had played no part in Greek democracy, and Roman women were not allowed to hold public office. Women's main role was to look after the home and raise children.

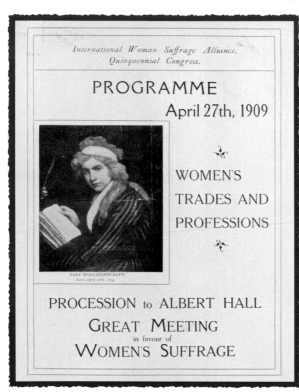

The writer Mary Wollstonecraft pictured on a suffrage meeting programme. Her most famous book was called A Vindication of the Rights of Women, published in 1792.

Inspired by the **French Revolution** of 1789, in which equality was one of the defining ideals, some **radicals** argued that women deserved the same rights as men. The pioneer English **feminist** Mary Wollstonecraft (1759-97) was a famous champion of women's rights. A character in her novel *The Wrongs of Women, or Maria* (1789) declares that the world is 'a vast prison and women born slaves'.

A few remarkable women succeeded even in a man's world. The nursing **reformer** Florence Nightingale (1820-1910) and the woman doctor Elizabeth Garrett Anderson (1836-1917) forged successful careers, despite opposition from men. But Florence Nightingale did not want the vote, saying she already had 'more political power than if I had been a borough returning two MPs'. Many better-off women, content with their comfortable lives, opposed votes for women, arguing that women did not have to 'compete' with men.

Women who did campaign for the vote formed **committees** and organised petitions for their cause, but in Parliament they had to ask men supporters to

In the 19th century, few middle-class women worked outside their homes. Poor women worked long hours for low wages – many of them as house servants like these 'domestics'.

speak for them. Men had to fight for the vote too. Even after three law changes (the Reform Acts of 1832, 1867 and 1884), not all men could vote in elections.

Peaceful protest

Education was the key to equality. By the mid-18th century, new schools for girls were sending women to study at universities and follow careers in teaching, business and medicine. As women's opportunities improved, the demand for suffrage grew. In the United States of America in 1848, a meeting of women led by Lucretia Mott and Elizabeth Cady Stanton called for the same voting rights as men. In 1872, American campaigner Susan B Anthony voted in the US presidential election: she was arrested for voting illegally.

Millicent Garrett Fawcett was the younger sister of Britain's first woman doctor, Elizabeth Garrett Anderson. In 1867, Millicent married a Liberal MP, Henry Fawcett (who was blind). He supported her campaign for votes for women.

In Britain, women **'suffragists'** pinned their hopes on persuading Parliament to change the law. Millicent Fawcett (1847-1929) was one. She was the wife of an MP, and a friend of the writer John Stuart Mill, also an MP, who argued strongly for women's votes. In 1867 Mrs Fawcett joined the first women's suffrage committee, formed two years before. Mill presented a petition to Parliament on the women's behalf, but their case was ignored.

Helen Taylor (1831-1907) was another suffrage committee member. Her mother Harriet was married to John Stuart Mill. Helen Taylor argued for women's rights, free schools for all and a fairer society. In 1885, she made a brave attempt to be elected as an MP. Her only meeting was broken up by opponents, and election officials told her to go home.

MILL'S LOGIC, OR FRANCHISE FOR FEMALES
"Pray clear the way, there, for these—ah—persons."

A magazine cartoon makes fun of John Stuart Mill and his support of franchise (the vote) for women. It also mocks suffragists for losing their femininity.

In 1897, Millicent Fawcett became president of the National Union of Women's Suffrage Societies. Under her leadership, the union continued to put forward its case for suffrage, but the British government continued to turn down voting reform, even though women in New Zealand had won the vote in 1893. Some suffragists began to worry that peaceful methods were getting nowhere.

The Pankhursts

The more **militant** campaigners found a leader in Emmeline Goulden. Born in 1858 in Manchester, she married a lawyer named Richard Pankhurst. Her husband supported Emmeline's work for women's rights to own property and belong to **trade unions**. After he died in 1898 Emmeline had to support herself, but with her daughters Christabel, Sylvia and Adela, she threw herself into the campaign for women's votes as a member of the North of England Society for Women's Suffrage.

Emmeline Pankhurst (left) in 1911, with her daughters Christabel (centre) and Sylvia (right). Emmeline came from a family with progressive views and found it hard to persuade women with more conservative backgrounds to join her cause.

Emmeline Pankhurst soon became impatient with the suffragists' lack of progress, believing they would not win the vote by gentle persuasion. She also felt that the leaders of the new Labour Party, who claimed to be in favour of women's rights, were not pushing hard enough for equality. So in 1903 she set up the Women's Social and Political Union (WSPU). The WSPU's motto was 'deeds, not words'. Some of its members were prepared to use limited violence to draw attention to the union's cause, including throwing eggs at politicians, setting fire to post boxes and chaining themselves to railings. They also believed that protesters should be ready to go to prison if necessary, to force the government to listen.

The more militant protesters were prepared to be arrested and many were.

Newspapers reported Mrs Pankhurst's speeches and WSPU demonstrations and the resulting publicity helped the suffragists' cause. But many women held back from joining the suffrage campaign, fearful of breaking the law or of upsetting their families. Moreover, few working women showed much interest in votes; their main concerns were improving their workplaces, which were often dangerous, shorter working hours and equal pay.

Suffragettes

Most of the 'votes for women' campaigners were middle-class people, from comfortable homes, and with time to spare. The Pankhursts realised that in order to strengthen their movement, they must win support from working women too. Lancashire-born millworker Annie Kenney (1879-1953) became a popular figurehead for the working women of the WSPU, appearing at meetings wearing her millworker's clothes, clogs and a shawl.

Annie Kenney in 1908. She joined the newly-formed WSPU in 1905 and rose quickly through its ranks to become the only working class woman to have a senior role in the organisation.

In 1905, Annie Kenney and Christabel Pankhurst attended a meeting in Manchester at which the foreign secretary was speaking. They shouted 'votes for women' and other slogans, and were thrown out. They were arrested after scuffling with police and sent to prison. The *Daily Mail* somewhat disparagingly called them *suffragettes* – and the name stuck.

The Pankhursts moved to London, where they met the wealthy activist Emmeline Pethick-Lawrence (1867-1954). Mrs Pethick-Lawrence took over running the WSPU's business affairs, leaving the Pankhursts more time to plan their next moves.

Mrs Pankhurst became a familiar figure speaking to large crowds in London and other cities, explaining why women must have the vote.

In April 1906, the Labour Party leader Keir Hardie proposed another 'votes for women' **bill**. It was defeated. In June 1906, a group of suffragettes met the Liberal Prime Minister, Henry Campbell-Bannerman. Emily Davies, a pioneer of women's education, told him that it had been 40 years since she had handed a women's rights petition to John Stuart Mill – and still nothing had been done. The prime minister told her women must be patient.

This was not what the suffragettes wanted to hear. In October 1906, 11 suffragettes were jailed for refusing to pay £10 fines after being arrested during a demonstration in the House of Lords. Mrs Pethick-Lawrence told the crowd defiantly: 'Women of England, we are going to prison for you, and therefore we do it gladly.'

Frustration mounts

From 1907 to 1914, the Pethick-Lawrences ran a suffragette newspaper called *Votes for Women*. Its readers were encouraged to read in March 1907 that women in Finland had won the vote – the first women voters in Europe. Yet back in Britain many suffragettes felt frustrated. Most MPs seemed content to let things go on as they were.

The suffragettes made good use of publicity to promote their cause. They published magazines and newspapers and even carried bags with eye–catching slogans.

In 1907 Emmeline Pankhurst organised a 'women's parliament' at Caxton Hall in London. From the meeting, a crowd of suffragettes marched to the House of Commons. Mounted police rode into the crowd, and some women were knocked down and hurt. Fifteen suffragettes got into the Commons building, where they were arrested. 'There can be no going back for us,' Mrs Pankhurst said bravely. Crowds cheered as the suffragettes were driven away to Holloway Prison.

Protests continued. Fifty suffragettes tried to smuggle themselves into Parliament inside a furniture van. Nine women were arrested for breaking into government ministers' homes. In 1908 Emmeline Pethick-Lawrence chained herself to the railings of 10 Downing Street, home of the prime minister. That summer, 200,000 people gathered for 'Women's Sunday' in London's Hyde Park, many wearing the purple, green and white sashes of the suffragette movement.

Such mass meetings showed that many people, including many men, were sympathetic to the suffragettes' cause. Yet although the Liberal government was ready to introduce some progressive reforms – such as Britain's first old-age pensions (1909) – it still refused to back a women's suffrage bill.

As this picture of 'Women's Sunday' shows, supporters of the suffragette movement came from all over Britain.

Cat and mouse

Women protesters faced rough treatment by police, and worse in prison. Their suffering increased public sympathy for their cause. The government offered vague promises of reform, and in 1910 the suffragettes called a truce during the general elections, hoping for success at last. Yet still nothing happened.

The March on London, 17 June 1911. Many suffragettes dressed as famous women from history, including Joan of Arc, Boudicca and Queen Elizabeth I.

In 1911, thousands of women marched in London. Some were dressed as famous women from history. Seven hundred marchers carried a silver arrow and a banner that read 'From prison to citizenship'. Each of these women had gone to prison for the suffragette cause.

In 1912, a new votes for women bill was defeated by 14 votes in the House of Commons. Angry suffragettes pointed out that men coal miners had been offered a minimum wage to settle a strike, but the government would not give women anything. The Pankhursts argued that this justified violent measures, such as breaking shop windows and even attacking MP's homes.

These actions do not seem so terrible in the modern world, but at the time people were shocked by such 'outrages'. The Pethick-Lawrences thought the Pankhursts were becoming too militant in their actions. They left the WSPU to set up their own independent organisation, the United Suffragists.

Some suffragettes in prison went on **hunger strike**. When they refused to eat, they were force-fed – a brutally painful medical procedure. In 1913, the government introduced the 'Cat and Mouse Act'. This

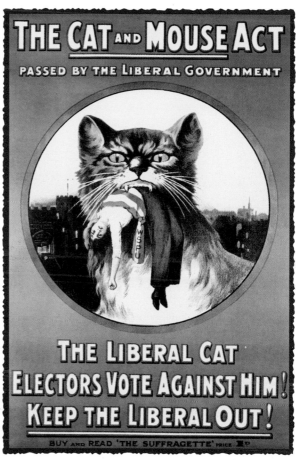

This poster of 1913 was inspired by the Cat and Mouse Act and urged voters to vote against the Liberal government.

law gave the police powers to arrest a suffragette, free her if she went on hunger strike and became ill, then arrest her again as soon as she was well. Many women went into hiding to avoid being caught, like 'mice'.

Tragedy at the Derby

Emily Davison, a university graduate, joined the WSPU in 1906. Considered extreme even by the more militant suffragettes, she was jailed several times for violent demonstrations. In prison, she showed a readiness for martyrdom, attempting to throw herself out of the window on two occasions.

A newspaper reports how suffragette Emily Davison flung herself in front of the king's horse during the 1913 Derby race.

In the summer of 1913, the racing season was in full swing. The Derby was the top horse race of the summer, and on 'Derby Day' people flocked to Epsom race course. King George V had a horse named Anmer running in the 1913 race.

Emily Davison also went to Epsom on 4 June, with a very public protest in mind. The race began, and the crowd cheered the jockeys on as they urged their horses around Tattenham Corner, a curve leading into the final straight. Suddenly, a woman dashed onto the course and tried to seize the reins of the king's horse. Horse and jockey fell. The other horses thundered past. The woman lay seriously injured.

Emily Davison died four days later. Her funeral procession in London on 14 June was attended by suffragettes wearing white, and watched by silent, thoughtful crowds.

Meanwhile, suffragette activity continued. In August, suffragettes tried to blow up government ministers' homes and others attacked Prime Minister Asquith on a golf course in Scotland. Mrs Pankhurst, now a fugitive, travelled to America, where she was at first refused entry as an 'undesirable'. She was later freed on the specific instructions of the US President Woodrow Wilson.

The funeral of Emily Davison became a suffragette demonstration on a huge scale.

Sympathy for the suffragette movement was growing worldwide. But time was running short for, in Europe, shadows were lengthening. War was coming.

23

Women at war

In the spring of 1914, suffragette Mary Richardson slashed a valuable painting called the *Rokeby Venus* in the National Gallery in London. She claimed she did it in protest at the government for valuing paintings of beautiful women more highly than the rights of real-life women. She also wanted to draw public attention to the government's treatment of Emmeline Pankhurst, 'the most beautiful character in modern history'.

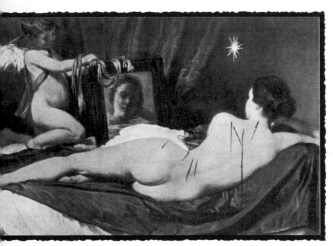

The **Rokeby Venus** *painting, by Velasquez, was slashed by a suffragette in 1914.*

In May 1914, Mrs Pankhurst was arrested outside Buckingham Palace. She and other suffragettes had been trying to present a petition, with over a million signatures of support, to King George V.

As the summer drew on, the government was more concerned with war fears. In August Britain went to war with Germany. The war was at first greeted with patriotic enthusiasm. The suffragettes suspended their campaign and the government freed all suffragettes from prison, calling on women to join the war effort. By 1918, nearly five million women were doing war work.

The war changed the image of women. In 1915, Edith Cavell, a British nurse working in German-occupied Belgium, was shot by the Germans for helping Allied soldiers escape capture. Though not a suffragette herself, Edith Cavell became a symbol of women's courage. Many other women, working in munitions factories or as nurses under shellfire, faced danger daily. So too did civilians at home, as bombing from the air brought the war to British cities.

Edith Cavell (1865-1915) came from Norfolk. A trained nurse, she worked at a hospital in Belgium from 1907 until the war began. She was executed by the German army in 1915.

Such courage and dedication made it impossible for the government to delay votes for women any longer. Women's suffrage became a 'war aim'. But the war dragged on for four long years, with mounting losses and many women spoke out against the senseless slaughter. Some called for an early peace.

Victory and votes

In December 1916, David Lloyd George became UK prime minister. Always more sympathetic than his predecessor, Asquith, to the suffragettes' cause, he soon held a conference to discuss the question of women's votes. There was no argument against now. On 28 March 1917, the House of Commons voted by 341 to 62 in favour of giving women over 30 the vote. Those entitled to vote were householders, the wives of householders, occupiers of property paying a minimum yearly rent of £5 and graduates of British universities. The change became law on 6 February 1918.

Cheering crowds celebrated the end of the war in November 1918, among them millions of women who would soon be able to vote.

Annie Kenney was overjoyed. She later wrote (in a book called *Memories of a Militant*) 'And so my suffrage pilgrimage was ended. Though I had no money, I had reaped a rich harvest of joy, laughter, romance, companionship and experience that no money can buy.'

The First World War ended in November 1918. Soon after came women's first chance to vote in a general election, held on 22 December 1918. The first woman elected to the British Parliament was Countess Markiewicz, but since she was a member of the Irish nationalist Sinn Fein party she refused to take her seat. In 1919, Lady Nancy Astor became the country's first woman MP, when she won a **by-election** at Plymouth.

Nancy Astor became Britain's first woman Member of Parliament in 1919.

In May 1928, the vote was given to all women over 21. Mrs Pankhurst, her suffragette battles won, planned to stand for Parliament as a Conservative, but she died in June 1928. In the election of 30 May 1929, millions of women over 21 voted for the first time and thirteen women were elected to Parliament. The suffragette's victory was complete.

Timeline

1792   Mary Wollstonecraft's book *A Vindication of the Rights of Women* published.

1848   Women's rights convention in the United States.

1865   Women's Suffrage Committee formed in Britain.

1867   Women in London collect 1,449 signatures on a votes for women petition, which John Stuart Mill presents to Parliament.

1869   Wyoming is the first US territory to give women the vote.

1885   Helen Taylor tries to stand for Parliament at North Camberwell, but election officials refuse to accept her as a candidate.

1886   First women's suffrage bill is proposed, but defeated. Five more will follow.

1893   Women in New Zealand get the vote.

1894   The Local Government Act gives women who are married to householders the right to vote in local government elections.

1896   *Daily Mail* is Britain's first 'popular' daily paper, with features designed to attract women readers.

1897   Millicent Fawcett is president of the new formed National Union of Women's Suffrage Societies (until 1918).

1903   The Women's Social and Political Union is formed in Manchester.

1905   Women's suffrage bill is 'talked out' (defeated). One MP said men and women had different 'mental equipment'.

1906	The Pankhursts move to London to continue the campaign.
1907	Finland is first country in Europe to give women the vote.
1908	*April* H H Asquith succeeds Henry Campbell-Bannerman as prime minister.
1908	*June* 200,000 suffragettes demonstrate in Hyde Park, London.
1912	Women in Norway get the vote.
1913	Asquith's voting reform bill is abandoned after opposition in Parliament to the 'women section'.
1914	*4 August* First World War begins: Germany invades Belgium.
1917	Russian Revolution: Mrs Pankhurst visits Russia and sees female soldiers of the 'Women's Death Battalion'.
1918	*11 November* First World War ends.
1918	*28 December* Women over 30 can vote, but only 17 of the 1600 candidates for Parliament are women.
1919	*1 December* Nancy Astor is first woman to take her seat as an elected MP.
1920	Women in the United States vote in the presidential election for the first time.
1924	First Labour government elected in Britain (January). Replaced by a Conservative government in October.
1928	*May 27* Equal Franchise Bill is passed unopposed. It gives women over 21 the vote.
1928	*June 14* Emmeline Pankhurst dies.
1929	*30 May* Women over 21 vote in the first election with universal over-21 suffrage. Thirteen women become MPs.

Glossary

bill A proposed law for discussion in Parliament; if agreed, it becomes law as an Act of Parliament.

by-election Election held when the MP for a place (a constituency) resigns or dies.

candidate A person seeking election to Parliament, or a position of any kind in competition with others.

committee Selected members of a group who are elected to represent the view of the group as a whole.

domestic servants Servants who work in people's homes, such as housemaids and cooks.

feminist A supporter of women's rights.

French Revolution The events from 1789-1799 when the French monarchy was overthrown and a new republic set up.

general election Election in Britain at which all members of the House of Commons are elected and a new government is formed.

hunger strike A protest in which a person refuses to eat or drink.

Industrial Revolution The change to mechanised factory-work that began in the late 18th century.

militant Someone with strongly held views, who may take a violent attitude towards those who oppose their ideas.

radical Someone with views on social change and reform that are usually in advance of what most people think possible or practical.

reformer Someone who tries to change things and improve life for other people.

suffragists Women campaigners for suffrage (the vote) who believed in peaceful protest.

trade unions Organisations of workers who act to secure better conditions and higher pay.

Who's Who

Nancy Astor (1879-1964) Became first woman Member of Parliament in 1919. A firm believer in the 'superiority of women', she remained an MP until 1945.

Margaret Bondfield (1873-1953) First woman to become a government minister (1924) and later to join the Cabinet (group of senior ministers).

Emily Davies (1830-1921) Pioneer campaigner for women's education.

Emily Wilding Davison (1872-1913) Joined the WSPU in 1906. Killed when she ran in front of a horse during the 1913 Derby.

Millicent Garrett Fawcett (1847-1929) Leading suffrage campaigner from 1867. Believed in non-violent action in support of votes for women.

Emmeline Pankhurst (born Goulden, 1858-1928) Most famous of all British suffragettes. Leader of the suffragette organisation the Women's Social and Political Union (founded 1903) and a lifelong campaigner for women's rights.

Annie Kenney (1879-1953) Lancashire-born mill-worker and trade unionist, who later became a suffragette. A close friend and ally of the Pankhursts.

Christabel Pankhurst (1880-1958) Eldest daughter of Emmeline Pankhurst, one of the first suffragettes to be arrested (with Annie Kenney) in 1905. Co-founder of the WSPU. Twice tried, and failed, to be elected as an MP.

Sylvia Pankhurst (1882-1960) Younger daughter of Mrs Pankhurst, active in the Labour Party. Worked in East London among working women.

Emmeline Pethick-Lawrence, (1867-1954) Treasurer of the WSPU and editor of the weekly paper *Votes for Women*. Later campaigned for women's welfare and international peace.

Index